AM2

11/17

The ABCs of
Thomas Merton

GREGORY RYAN & ELIZABETH RYAN

A Monk at the Heart of the World

PARACLETE PRESS
BREWSTER, MASSACHUSETTS

For all the loving sisters:
Caitlin & Abigail
and
Charlotte & Grace

2017 First Printing

The ABCs of Thomas Merton: A Monk at the Heart of the World

Copyright © 2017 by Gregory J. Ryan and Elizabeth H. Ryan

ISBN 978-1-61261-847-0

The art work for the letter "D" is based on a photograph of Thomas Merton and the Dalai Lama from the collections of the Thomas Merton Center at Bellarmine University. Used with permission.

The Paraclete Press name and logo (dove on cross) are trademarks of Paraclete Press, Inc.

Library of Congress Cataloging-in-Publication Data

Names: Ryan, Gregory, author, illustrator. | Ryan, Elizabeth (Elizabeth H.),
    author, illustrator.
Title: The ABCs of Thomas Merton : a monk at the heart of the world /
    written and illustrated by Gregory and Elizabeth Ryan.
Description: Brewster, Massachusetts : Paraclete Press, 2017.
Identifiers: LCCN 2016050921 | ISBN 9781612618470 (hardback)
Subjects: LCSH: Merton, Thomas, 1915-1968--Miscellanea--Juvenile literature.
Classification: LCC BX4705.M542 R93 2017 | DDC 271/.12502--dc23
LC record available at https://lccn.loc.gov/2016050921

10 9 8 7 6 5 4 3 2 1

Published by Paraclete Press
Brewster, Massachusetts
www.paracletepress.com

Printed in Malaysia

Thomas Merton was a Trappist monk, an artist and a writer. He was born in France, but lived most of his life in the United States. His parents, Ruth and Owen, were also artists. After college, he felt that God was calling him to love the world by living a life of prayer. He joined a monastery in Kentucky so he could live, pray, and work with other monks. With his brother monks, Merton learned to love God, the earth, and all people. He became a monk at the heart of the world.

A is for abbot. The abbot is the monk in charge of the whole monastery. He cares for all the monks who live there. He is their teacher and spiritual father. When the monastery needs a new abbot, the monks elect one.

Thomas Merton's first abbot was Abbot Frederic Dunne. His second abbot was Abbot James Fox. His last abbot was Abbot Flavian Burns, who had been one of Merton's students.

B is for Saint Benedict who lived in Italy about 1500 years ago. Monks live by the Rule he wrote for monasteries. It is a rule of love. Its message is peace—"Pax!" in Latin. Thomas Merton lived by this rule for 27 years.

B is for bread. Bread for the altar and bread for the dinner table. Monks live on both kinds of bread.

C is for cowl. A cowl is a monk's long white robe with a hood. Thomas Merton's cowl covered him from the top of his head to the tops of his shoes. The cowl is worn at prayer times and wraps the monk in silence.

C is for community. We all find God's love and mercy within ourselves and in the people around us—our families, our neighborhoods, our towns and nations. Merton found his community at Gethsemani, his community of love.

D is for Dalai Lama. The Dalai Lama is the leader of the people of Tibet. Merton visited with him in India a short time before Merton died. The Dalai Lama has said that when he thinks of the word "Christian" he thinks of Thomas Merton. The Dalai Lama's message is for peace among all people. That was Thomas Merton's message, too.

E is for England. When Tom was thirteen, he left France, where he was an excellent student, to live and study at a boarding school in England. He started college there, too, but finished at Columbia University in New York City.

F is for Fire Watch and Fire Tower. The monks take turns staying awake during the night to watch for fires in and around the monastery. Outside in the woods there is a fire tower where Thomas Merton used to climb high above the trees to watch for forest fires. He prayed there, too, alone in nature with God.

F is for France. Thomas Merton was born to Ruth Jenkins Merton (an American) and Owen Merton (a New Zealander) in Prades, France, on January 31, 1915. When he was about a year and a half old, they all went to live with his mother's family in America.

G is for Gandhi. Mahatma Gandhi was a holy man in India. Merton studied Gandhi's life and writings and learned more about how all people should live and work together in peace. He even wrote a book about Gandhi.

G is for Gethsemani Abbey. When he was 26 years old, Thomas Merton went to Kentucky and became a Trappist monk of the Abbey of Our Lady of Gethsemani. The monastery was started by monks who had come from France in 1848. Those first monks cut down trees for lumber to build the monastery. They farmed the land to grow their own food. Today, the monks make and sell fruitcake and fudge to support themselves. About 35 monks live at Gethsemani today.

H is for hermitage. For the last three years of his life, Merton lived alone in a little cabin in the woods of the monastery. A person who lives alone with God is called a hermit. The house they live in is called a hermitage. Merton's hermitage was named "Our Lady of Carmel." He named it in honor of Mary, the Mother of God. He prayed, worked, and wrote books in the hermitage. He also spent a lot of time walking and praying alone in the woods surrounding the hermitage.

I is for Ishi. Thomas Merton studied the ways of Native American Indians. He wrote a book about them and named it "Ishi Means Man."

J is for Jesus. Merton felt that Jesus had called him to leave his life outside in the world and to live the rest of his life inside the monastery. Everything Merton did was because of his love for Jesus and for other people.

J is for Jonas, a prophet in the Bible. Merton named one of his books *The Sign of Jonas* because he thought God was always bringing surprises into his life—just as He did with Jonas.

K is for Martin Luther King Jr. Martin was a
Baptist minister in the southern United States who worked
in a nonviolent way for the rights of African Americans.
He had a dream that one day all people would live together
as one big family. Thomas Merton admired Dr. King and
shared his dream.

L is for Louis. When Merton became a monk, he changed his name from Thomas to Louis because from that day on, he would be a "new man." The other monks called him Father Louis. The younger monks, whom he taught, nicknamed him "Uncle Louie."

M is for monastery. A monastery is a place where monks live, work, and pray together. They try to follow the Gospel message of Jesus. Everything they need is in the monastery: food, clothing, medicine, books—and most importantly, their own church. Some monks are priests. Thomas Merton was a priest at Gethsemani. He was very happy to have a chapel in his hermitage where he could say Mass each day.

N is for nature. From when he was a young boy, Thomas Merton loved spending time in nature. Much of his most beautiful writing, photos, and art work is about the trees, flowers, birds, and deer that lived in the woods around the monastery and around his hermitage.

N is for nonviolence. This is a way to help do away with violence in the world—with the power of love. Gandhi, Martin Luther King Jr. and Thomas Merton all preached nonviolence to everyone in the world: "Love one another." Just as Jesus told us to do.

O is for obedience. Monks do not live only for themselves. They promise to live in obedience to their abbot, to each other, and to God. Merton felt that obedience would help him to love everyone more because he would think more about them and less about himself.

P is for poetry. Thomas Merton was an artist who made art in different ways—sometimes with ink and brushes, sometimes with a camera, but most of the time with words. He wrote sixty books. Many of them were books of poetry. His art brought him closer to God and brought God closer to him.

P is for peace. Merton's whole life as a monk was spent bringing more peace into the world. With his art, his prayer, his friendships, his books—with everything he did.

P is for prayer. Thomas Merton spent long hours in prayer each day. He prayed while reading the Bible. Seven times a day, all the monks came together in church—to chant and pray and celebrate Mass. Merton also spent time alone in silent meditation. His writing and his time spent outdoors in nature were also prayer for him. Everything he did kept him in God's presence.

Q is for Mary, Queen of Heaven. Mary's life
as the loving mother of Jesus is a model for us to follow.
As she lived with her son, Jesus, she kept all his teachings
in her heart. And so should we. Monks end each day by
singing a hymn to Mary called the "Salve Regina"—"Hail,
Holy Queen. . . ."

R is for races of people—red, brown, yellow, white, or black. Thomas Merton wrote that we should all live together in peace and help one another as children of God, no matter what color we are.

S is for silence and solitude. A person seeking God needs time alone for peace and quiet. Father Louis lived "alone with God" and with his brother monks. He hardly ever left his monastery, though visitors from around the world sometimes came to share in his silence and solitude.

is for Trappist. The monks in Thomas Merton's monastery belong to a very old order called Cistercians of the Strict Observance. They are called Trappists, for short—named after La Trappe, one of their famous monasteries in France. Trappists live a very simple and quiet life of prayer, study, and work. Outside of their prayer times together in church, they spend their waking and sleeping hours in silence.

U is for Universe. Merton believed that the whole universe is "alive" with God's presence. God's love is everywhere—in nature and in people—if we just look for it.

V is for Vespers. Monks leave their chores around the monastery and come to the church to sing God's praise. They gather together in the middle of the night, very early in the morning, and a few other times during the day. Their evening prayer is called Vespers.

W is for war. Thomas Merton said war should be outlawed. "War should be gone from the planet." Amen!

W is for wisdom. Wisdom is a way of knowing not with your head but with your heart, your whole self. Merton wrote a wonderful poem about wisdom. He called it "Hagia Sophia," which is Greek for Holy Wisdom.

X is for Christos (χριστός), the Greek word for Messiah or the Anointed One. Jesus "Christ" comes from this word. Merton ended many of his letters with the words "in the love of Christ" or "in Xto" for short.

Y is for Lee Ying. Merton saw a photograph of her in a magazine. Lee Ying was trying to leave Communist China so she could make a new home and "live free" in Hong Kong. But instead of being welcomed in Hong Kong, she was sent back to China. Instead of smiling and being happy, Lee Ying was crying her eyes out! Reading about her and seeing how unhappy she was broke Merton's heart. The whole world was sad for her. Merton wrote a poem about her called "A Picture of Lee Ying."

Z is for Zen. Zen comes from Asia. It is a way of seeing the world just as things are. Like the sun shining brightly in the heavens. Or the songs of the birds in the trees. Thomas Merton's Zen made him a better Christian monk and helped him to love God, nature, all men and women, and girls and boys.

Thomas Merton—Fr. M. Louis Merton, OCSO—
died in Bangkok, Thailand, on December 10, 1968. He
had gone there to speak at an important meeting of monks
and nuns gathered from all over the world. Instead of
returning to be with his brother monks at Gethsemani, he
went home to God in heaven.

At Gethsemani Abbey, a simple white cross marks where
Merton's body rests—just like those of all his brother
monks who died before him.

May he rest in peace.

A Note to Parents and Teachers

In his address to the United States Congress on September 24, 2015, Pope Francis talked about four outstanding Americans. One of them was Thomas Merton. The Pope said, "[Thomas Merton] remains a source of spiritual inspiration and a guide for many people. . . . Merton was above all a man of prayer, a thinker who challenged the certitudes of his time and opened new horizons for souls and for the Church. He was also a man of dialogue, a promoter of peace between peoples and religions."

In this little book, your child or student will learn the "big ideas" about Thomas Merton (1915–1968), or Father Louis, as he was known at the Abbey of Gethsemani, nestled in the hills of Kentucky. It is by no means a biography.

Merton was a prolific writer, first as he lived the normal life of a monk in community with his fellow monks, and then in a hermitage on the grounds of his monastery, where he lived a life of greater solitude, silence, and prayer.

Merton published sixty books during his lifetime, with many others published after his death. He wrote about his own life in *The Seven Storey Mountain* and in his published journals and letters. He maintained a vast correspondence with men and women in all walks of life all over the world. Numerous full-length biographies, as well as audio and video materials, are available in bookstores and online.

To learn more, visit:

The Thomas Merton Center: www.merton.org

The International Thomas Merton Society (ITMS):
www.merton.org/ITMS

The Abbey of Gethsemani: www.monks.org

Christian Meditation for Children: www.cominghome.org.au

For more information or to subscribe to *The Merton Seasonal* quarterly contact:

The Thomas Merton Center
2001 Newburg Road
Louisville, Kentucky 40205
Tel. 502-272-8177 or 8187

The authors are grateful to Paul Pearson, Patrick O'Connell, and Bonnie Thurston
for their helpful suggestions in the preparation of this book,
and to Brother Patrick Hart, OCSO, and Robert Lax for their encouragement and
enthusiasm—from A to Z!